W9-AET-707

MINNESOTA BUG HUNT

Text by Bruce Giebink

Photographs by Bill Johnson

www.mhspress.org

Manufactured in Canada

10 9 8 7 6 5 4 3 2 1

The paper used in this publication meets the minimum requirements of the American National Standard for Information Sciences—Permanence for Printed Library Materials, ANSI Z39.48-1984.

International Standard Book Number
ISBN: 978-0-87351-865-9 (cloth)

Library of Congress Cataloging-in-Publication Data

Giebink, Bruce.
Minnesota bug hunt / Bruce Giebink, Bill Johnson.
p. cm.
ISBN 978-0-87351-865-9 (cloth : alk. paper)
1. Insects—Minnesota—Juvenile literature.
2. Insects—Minnesota—Identification—Juvenile literature.
3. Insects—Minnesota—Pictorial works. I. Johnson, Bill, 1948– II. Title.
QL475.M6G54 2013
595.7—dc23

2012044590

We're Going on a Bug Hunt!

BUGS (insects and other assorted creepy-crawly critters) are everywhere. They come in an almost endless variety of shapes, colors, and sizes. Most of them we seldom see because they live in a hidden and mysterious world— a world we only get a glimpse of now and then.

To find as many different kinds (or **species**) of insects as possible, it's important to explore different habitats. A **habitat** is the home where a particular insect, animal, or plant lives, like a grassland, a wooded area, a pond, an oak tree, or your own backyard.

If you're curious about the kinds of bugs that live in and around Minnesota, this book is for you. Get ready for a close-up and personal peek at some of Minnesota's more interesting and unusual six-legged residents.

We hope this book makes you excited about bugs and nature and encourages you to get out and explore the world of bugs on your own.

Backyard Habitat

Just how "buggy" is your backyard or nearby park? What six-legged critters are you likely to find hiding out there? Every backyard has places for bugs to hang out: on flowers, trees, and bushes, or under rocks and logs.

Yikes! Look at those pincers! Can they pinch? Sure, they can give you a painful pinch, but only if mishandled. **Earwigs** use their **pincers** (which are actually **cerci**, or tails) to protect themselves and their young. They also use them for grabbing and holding weak or dead insects, which they then eat. Female earwigs are protective mothers who guard and defend their eggs and young.

EARWIG

The name *earwig* comes from the ancie[nt] belief that these insec[ts] would crawl into sleeping people's ears and bore into their brain, causing insanity. NOT true! T[he] name also refers to their small hind wing[s,] which are shaped like little ears, hence "earwi(n)g."

Aha! There it is! Most of the time, the **Jagged Ambush Bug** is so well camouflaged that you don't notice it. Its **camouflage** (disguise) allows it to **ambush** (sneak up on) its **prey**—the insects it eats. It grabs its prey with special "bug-grabbing" front legs. This feisty little predator often captures insects much larger than itself, even bumblebees ten times its size! Its secret weapon is poison saliva, which paralyzes its prey in seconds.

JAGGED AMBUSH BUG

Look for the jagged ambush bug on yellow flowers. Can you see it here, next to the Green Bottle Fly?

Pop goes the weasel! ***Click*** goes the beetle! **Click Beetles** really do *click*—right before they flip. If this beetle falls on its back, it first bends its head back. Then, with a sudden jerk and ***click***, it straightens out its body and flips into the air, spinning end over end, landing right side up. At night, look for click beetles flying around lights.

LOCUST BORER BEETLE

This bug is a **Locust Borer Beetle**. It looks like a wasp, but it's really a kind of longhorn beetle. Since it looks like a bee, it's hoping you'll leave it alone. The best place to find it is on goldenrod in the fall.

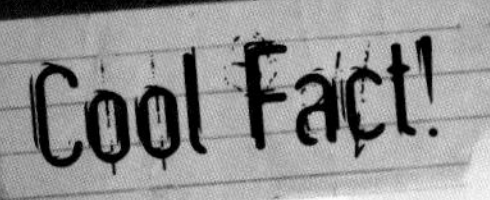

The locust borer gets its name because the larvae **bore**, or drill, into locust trees.

ELM BORER BEETLE

Check out the eyes and "feelers" on this cute bug! The **Elm Borer Beetle**'s eyes are so large and dark it almost seems to be wearing sunglasses. Notice the compound eyes. **Compound eyes** are made up of many small simple eyes, called **ommatidia**. The more ommatidia an insect has, the better it is at detecting movement and seeing details. This beetle gets its name because of its larvae, which bore into the wood of elm trees.

Cool Fact!

The dragonfly, which is an excellent flyer and predator, has as many as 48,000 ommatidia in EACH compound eye!

RI-COLORED BUMBLE BEE

How can such a large bee with such small wings fly? This is a **Tri-colored Bumble Bee**. Its dense blanket of hairs helps to insulate it and warm up its body, even on chilly days.

Cool Fact!

The body temperature of an active bumblebee can be much higher than the actual air temperature, making the bee almost **warm-blooded**. For this reason, bumblebees are able to fly in much cooler temperatures than most **pollinators**.

Grassland Prairie Habitat

Grassy areas, especially those with plenty of wildflowers, are excellent habitats for bugs. As you wander SLOWLY through a grassy field, look and listen carefully. Most likely, you'll SEE the most bug activity around patches of wildflowers. But if you're listening carefully, you'll HEAR a chorus of insect sounds (buzzing, chirping, rasping) all around you. No shortage of bugs here!

Cool Fact!

In the air, the Carolina Locust's bright black-and yellow-banded wings make it very noticeable. B when resting on the ground, it's extremely well camouflaged and nearly impossible to see.

CAROLINA LOCUST

Ever see a grasshopper hover, like a helicopter? Or hear one make loud crackling and snapping sounds as it flies away? Well, the **Carolina Locust** does just that! When it's looking for a mate, the male flutters and hovers like a butterfly. The loud crackling and snapping sounds it makes during flight are called **crepitations**.

ROAD-WINGED KATYDID

tice the **antennae** on this **Broad-winged Katydid**. Katydids have
g, hair-like antennae. When a male katydid wants to communicate with
emale, he sings to her. His "song" is a raspy sound that he produces by
bbing his forewings together. The female "hears" his song with an
gan on her foreleg called a **tympanum**.

Meadow Spittlebugs are the bubble-making champs of the bug world! Those foamy blobs you sometimes see on plants are produced by these tiny bugs, which belong to a group of insects called **froghoppers**. Actually, the **nymphs** (babies) are the real bubble-makers. By hiding in these frothy bubbles, **meadow spittlebugs** protect themselves from their enemies and from drying out.

MEADOW SPITTLEBUG

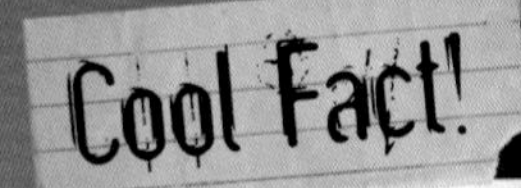

Spittlebugs mix air with a fluid they secrete. They whip the air bubbles into froth with little fingers at the tip of their abdomen.

BLISTER BEETLE

This beetle doesn't look very threatening, does it? It would be best not to pick it up, though. The **Blister Beetle** has a secret chemical weapon called **cantharidin**. Cantharidin causes blisters on the skin and makes these beetles poisonous to eat.

IREFLY

reflies are fascinating, agical insects. Their blinking is ore than just a light show—it's like any songs being sung in different languages. ore than twelve different species of fireflies live Minnesota. Each has its own special "light song." ew species are only active in the daytime and

Cool Fact!

The larvae of all firefly species ... called **glowworms**.

ROBBER FLY

This big, hairy bug looks a lot like a bumblebee, but it's not a bee at all. It's **Robber Fly**. Robber flies are fast, sha eyed predators that constantly scan the for their next meal. Once they spot their victim, they zoom after it, grab it in mid ride it to the ground, and eat it. These je fighters of the insect world will attack pr insects of any size, including large bees.

Cool Fact!

Some species of robber flies like to eat honeybees. They'll hang around beehives and pick off the bees as they come and go. When more people kept bees to make honey, robberflies basically "robbed" beekeepers of their bees.

Milkweed plants are loaded with **toxic** (poisonous) chemicals, which is why only a few insects are able to feed on them. Those that can—like the monarch butterfly and this **Red Milkweed Beetle**—are brightly colored to warn predators that they taste bad.

Forest Habitat

Forests are cool and damp and provide food and shelter for a wide variety of insects. Mature forests with lots of different trees and sunny clearings are excellent places for you to hunt bugs.

CECROPIA MOTH

Wow! Look at this awesome moth! With a wingspan of four to six inches, the **Cecropia Moth** is the largest and one of the most beautiful moths you'll find in Minnesota. Look for them flying around lights late at night or resting nearby.

A full-grown Cecropia caterpillar is covered with yellow, blue, and red knobs (called **tubercles**) and can grow to a length of four inches.

MOURNING CLOAK BUTTERFLY

Want to know what's so special about this common **Mourning Cloak Butterfly**? First, it's the only butterfly in Minnesota that spends the winter as an adult (most spend the winter as a **chrysalis** and a few spend it as a caterpillar). That's why it's the first butterfly we see in the spring. Second, it's one of our longest living butterflies. Adults can survive almost an entire year.

Cool Fact!

Look for this spiny black and red caterpillar on mainly willows and poplars, but also on elm, hackberry, and birch leaves.

The caterpillars of **Geometrid Moths** are called **inchworms** because they loop or inch forward rather than crawl. Many inchworms are also masters of disguise and can "disappear" when danger threatens. They do this by freezing their bodies at a stiff angle so they look more like a twig than a caterpillar.

GEOMETRID MOTH

Inchworms loop along because they don't have a middle pair of legs (called **prolegs**). Some species look like pine needles. Others have bumps and swellings like leaf buds or leaf scars.

VIRGIN TIGER MOTH

Look at this colorful beauty! It's almost too colorful to be a moth, right? But it IS a moth, a **Virgin Tiger Moth**. Its bright colors and bold patterns are a warning to predators that it tastes bad.

NORTHEASTERN SAWYER BEETLE

Look at that face! Check out those antennae! This curious-looking bug is a **Northeastern Sawyer Beetle**. This long-horned, wood-boring beetle has antennae longer than its body.

Cool Fact!

Sawyer beetle larvae feed by boring into dying spruce and balsam fir trees.

Bizarre bug alert!

What insect has a front end like a praying mantis and a back end like a lacewing? Answer: the **Mantisfly**. Like a mantis, its large front legs are specially designed for capturing and holding prey. Its wings have a shape and vein pattern similar to a lacewing's.

MANTISFLY

Cool Fact!

Mantisflies also have a crazy **life cycle**. Their larvae live either as parasites of spider egg sacs or predators of beetle, moth, or wasp larvae. Mantisfly larvae will not rest until they find a spider egg sac to live in or some kind of larva to devour. Once the feeding begins, they become sluggish, barely moving couch potatoes.

Pond Habitat

Minnesota is home to lots of lakes and ponds. It's easy to find a variety of insects both in and around the water. All have special **adaptations** for living in or on the water.

Cool Fact!

The dragonfly's **aquatic** larvae have the craziest creature features. Their specially designed mouth can rapidly extend to grab prey as it swims by. And they can squirt water out of their back end to rapidly propel themselves through the water for short distance

Minnesota has many species of dragonflies, but the **Common Green Darner Dragonfly** is unique. Every fall it **migrates** from Minnesota to Texas and other southern states. It's also the first dragonfly that we see flying in Minnesota in the spring.

COMMON GREEN DARNER DRAGONFLY

Cool Fact!

Dragonflies can have as many as 48,000 ommatidia (single eyes) in EACH of their compound eyes, making them very good at finding and catching other flying insects.

TWELVE-SPOTTED SKIMMER DRAGONFLY

This **Twelve-Spotted Skimmer Dragonfly** gets its name from the twelve black spots on its wings. Skimmers alternate between taking short, rapid flights over ponds and perching on nearby twigs and grass. They choose a favorite perch to use as a home base and return to it often. Like many dragonflies, the skimmer will travel a long way from water.

GIANT WATER BUG

Believe it or not, this giant of a bug is probably living in a pond near you. The **Giant Water Bug** is one of the largest insects in Minnesota. It can be two and a half inches long. These bugs are referred to as "toe biters" because they feed in plants and in the muck along the bottoms of ponds and lakes—just where your toes might be.

Cool Fact!

Even though water bugs live in ponds and lakes, you're more likely to find them in well-lit areas like ball fields, parking lots, and tennis courts. They're often called "electric light bugs" for this reason.

WATER STRIDER

Thanks to their special feet, **Water Striders** can walk on water. The feet (or **tarsi**) on their middle and hind legs have a thick covering of water-repellent hairs. These hairs allow the striders to skate over the water's surface.

Cool Fact!

The water strider's legs also have ripple-sensitive hairs. These hairs alert them to other insects struggling on the surface. The striders capture those insects with short front legs built for grabbing prey.

WATER BOATMAN

Another insect specially designed for life in the water is the **Water Boatman**. Its body is smooth and flat. Its oar-like back legs quickly propel it through the water.

Most of the time, the water boatman breathes at the water's surface. But it can also spend time underwater by carrying a bubble of air under its wings and around its abdomen, much like a scuba diver.

Cool Fact!

Oak Tree Habitat

average oak tree rovides food and shelter or nearly three hundred pecies of insects. That s an amazing number of DIFFERENT KINDS of insects on a single tree. They range in size from tiny gall wasps and leaf miners to giant hungry caterpillars of silk moths like the Polyphemus.

Cool Fact!

Polyphemus moths communicate with chemicals. Females give off a chemical signal called a **pheromone** to let males know they are in the area. Males detect this chemical signal with their large, feathery antennae. You can tell the males from the females because the male's antennae are much larger.

POLYPHEMUS MOTH

Oak leaves are a favorite food of **Polyphemus** caterpillars. The Polyphemus moth has a large blue and yellow **eyespot** on each hind wing. The eyespots are hidden by the front wings when the moth is resting. But if you startle this moth, it will quickly spread its forewings, suddenly "flashing" the eyespots on its hind wings as it tries to startle you back.

Cool Fact!

Weevils use their snouts, which have mouthparts at the end, to bore into acorns so they can lay eggs inside.

ACORN WEEVIL

Weevils belong to a huge family of beetles with **snouts**. They are among the most common insects on earth. Their snouts may be short and stubby or long and skinny. The snout on this **Acorn Weevil** is long, about as long as its body.

CHECKERED FRINGE PROMINENT CATERPILLAR

It may look like a dead, curled-over leaf, but it's really the **Checkered Fringe Prominent Caterpillar**. When it turns into a moth, it will camouflage itself by pretending to be a twig stub. It does this by rolling its wings and resting with its head down and wings pointing up.

OAK LACE BUG

This pretty little bug is the **Oak Lace Bug**. Its body and wings are sculpted, giving it a lacey appearance. Look for oak lace bugs on the undersides of oak leaves. They feed in groups, so if you find one, you're likely to find more nearby.

Insects come in an almost endless variety of shapes, colors, and sizes. They look so different from us that they seem like alien creatures. Most live in their own hidden, mysterious world, just waiting for you to discover them!

You can find bugs almost everywhere. But if you want to find **LOTS** of **DIFFERENT SPECIES** of bugs, you need to keep some important things in mind.

- In Minnesota (and nearby northern states), the best time of year to look for bugs is from mid-June through mid-September. **Explore different habitats, like grasslands, forests, and ponds.**

- Plants provide food and homes for different kinds of insects. **During your bug hunt, check out lots of different plants.** For example, flowers are very important to many insects. Flowers produce **nectar,** the high-energy fuel that powers many active insects such as bees, wasps, and butterflies. To these bugs, flowers are like fast-food, drive-through restaurants! A patch of wildflowers on a warm, sunny day is an ideal place to start any bug hunt.

- **Slow down and look carefully.** Some insects are easy to find because they are big, colorful, and active during the day, like monarch butterflies and bumblebees. But most insects live in a hidden world, and you need to look carefully to find them. Many are masters of disguise and blend in with their surroundings. Many you'll hear but not see, like crickets, katydids, and cicadas. Others are under or inside logs, beneath rocks, or in the soil itself. You'll miss them if you don't look carefully! So slow down and be patient.

One of the best ways to find insects hiding in grass and bushes is to get a good sturdy net and sweep it back and forth through the plants. Then dump everything you catch in the net on a large white sheet or piece of cardboard. You'll be surprised to see what's living in just a small patch of weeds or flowers.

To my wife, Lisa, who has enabled me to pursue my passion for insects and to share my knowledge and enthusiasm with audiences of all ages, especially children. And to my son and daughter, Cameron and Anna: may you both find a passion as rich and rewarding as mine has been. —B.G.

To longtime friend and supporter of my photography Kathy Ludwig. —B.J.

About the Author

Entomologist **Bruce Giebink**—better known as **Bruce the Bug Guy**—offers activities for children of all ages through his company the **Bug Zone**. Learn more at www.brucethebugguy.net.

About the Photographer

Award-winning photographer **Bill Johnson**'s work is featured in many publications, including in the *Kaufman Field Guide to Insects of North America* and in his *Horticulture Magazine* column, "**Insect ID**," as well as at his website: www.billjohnsonbeyondbutterflies.com.